Thoughts from Erica's Pastor.....

I was honored to be asked to write a few thoughts for Erica as she has become like a sister to me over the past several years. I first met Erica when I came to The Living Stone Church in 2012. Since then I have watched her love for Jesus grow and become a driving force in her life. At times she can be quite timid, but these are rare times, as her faith is too strong to be subdued for very long. Knowing how strong she is, as her "older brother," I like to torment her and pose questions that cause her to stop dead in her tracks as she decides if she is on track or not, to which she generally responds with something along the lines of, "My confidence is in God."

This 21 Day Devotional is an inspiring example of extreme confidence in God, mixed with the doubts and limitations of our human mind. Each day's devotion stands on its own as Erica encourages us through example and then compels us to "Pause, Ponder and Pray," yet this work as a whole is designed to draw us all closer to Jesus so that we can live in His love.

As I read each day's devotion, I could hear Erica's voice in the words and could sense her sincere desire that God be glorified and that each reader would know how much Jesus loves them and that He desires to train and enable us to "*throw off everything that hinders and the sin that so easily entangles. And let us run with perseverance the race marked out for us.*" Hebrews 12:1

The next 21 Days will change your perception as you draw closer to God and just might be the motivation you've been searching for to run this race called life!

Pastor Eric Alwine
The Living Stone
Rossville In.

DRAWING NEAR TO GOD

A 21 DAY CHALLENGE

ERICA WALLACE

Erica Wallace
Hebrews 4:16

Printed by Kindle Direct Publishing,
An Amazon.com Company

Erica@ExpectToSeeGodToday.org
ExpectToSeeGodToday.org

Book design by Eric Dean | ejdcreative.com

ISBN: 978-1-7273338-1-7

Acknowledgement

There are so many people who made this devotional happen. First, I'm thankful for the nudge of the Holy Spirit to do something. This devotional was an outpouring of the Holy Spirit, a gift. Secondly for all the many people who let me bounce my ideas off them, for their feedback and encouragement, when I wanted to quit. To those who worked on editing with me, your patience and dedication was greatly appreciated. To my prayer warriors who covered me in prayer during this process. Prayer made this happen "in His time" and allowed me to rest in that assurance.

To my husband, my rock and my unsung hero. I could not do what I do, without your continual love and support.

I do want to personally say, "Thank you" to Pastor Eric. Thank you for continually challenging me to grow in my relationship with Christ. Thank you for carefully tearing my work apart to see if it stood up to the teachings that I was trying to express. Your investment in this project was very much appreciated and "thank you" hardly seems enough.

Dedication

This devotional is dedicated to anyone who knows the Lord as their personal Lord and Savior and wants to have a closer relationship with Him.

Table of Contents

Introduction

For Christmas 2016 I received the book, "21 Days of Prayer for Your Business — Making God the Foundation of Your Journey" by Monique McLean.

As I read this book/workbook it challenged the way I thought about prayer because it changed my perspective. Although this book was written with a business in mind, I applied it to my life. It caused me to draw closer to God and that book coupled with a few other books, led to a changed way of praying. It became more of a lifestyle instead of something I do in the morning or at night or any other certain time of day.

God continually has each of us on a journey. Some days it's smooth sailing, other days we can hardly put one foot in front of the other. But regardless of the day, God is the same. He loves each of us more than we can imagine. Part of my journey was training for a mini-marathon. I wasn't even sure why I signed up, I just knew I was supposed to. Now, I believe it was for the purpose of bringing forth this 21-day challenge.

Please join me on these next 21 days as I share part of my story with you. Sharing one's story can be hard, so please read each day with tender care. There will be follow up questions, that if you allow, will help you in your growth. Before jumping into the questions, pause and pray. My prayer for you is that see yourself sitting and talking with Jesus as you work through the questions. Ask the Holy Spirit to open your heart and eyes to things you would rather not see. The questions are general but be specific in your answers.

These next 21 days could just be another 21 days of interesting reading, or it could be the 21 days of a change in your life that begins in your heart. The choice is yours. So, grab a notebook, jot down the date of the day you start so when you look back in 6 months or even a year, it will be easier to gauge your growth. Hopefully at the end of the 21 days you will have started on a journey that is truly, just the beginning. I will be praying for you during these next 21 days, that you and God will draw closer together during this time. That He starts you on a new and exciting journey of seeking Him more, since there is always more of Jesus to be had!

Blessings,
Erica Wallace

DAY 1

The Cross

"For the message of the cross is foolishness to those who are perishing, but to us who are being saved it is the power of God."
1 CORINTHIANS 1:18 NIV

Before we step into the next 21 days, we need to start on level ground, and that ground is the cross! To those who don't know Christ, the cross seems to be foolishness. 1 Corinthians 1:23-24 says it better than I can, *"but we preach Christ crucified: a stumbling block to Jews and foolishness to Gentiles, but to those whom God has called, both Jews and Greeks, Christ the power of God and the wisdom of God."*

God has a call on each of our lives. If you don't know Christ as your Savior, then the call is a call of salvation, to trust Him with your eternal soul. To be able to know, beyond a shadow of a doubt, that if you were to die today you would stand in the presence of Christ our Lord. Let's walk through Romans 10:9-13.

"If you declare with your mouth, "Jesus is Lord," and believe in your heart that God raised him from the dead, you will be saved. For it is with your heart that you believe and are justified, and it is with your mouth that you profess your faith and are saved. As Scripture says,

"Anyone who believes in him will never be put to shame." For there is no difference between Jew and Gentile — the same Lord is Lord of all and richly blesses all who call on him, for, "Everyone who calls on the name of the Lord will be saved."

See the Cross is foolishness to those that don't recognize their need for the atonement of their sin or that sin separates us from God. Yet, God didn't turn his back on us, he loved us enough to send his Son, Jesus, to be that perfect sacrifice on the cross for us. God overcame death when Jesus died on the cross. Jesus didn't just die he rose on the 3rd day, overcoming the grave!

If you believe Jesus is the Son of God and died for you, it is as 1 Corinthians 1:18 says, *"...to us being saved it is the power of God."* This power, the power of the Holy Spirit, is what's going to help you walk and grow on your 21-day journey.

Pause, Ponder and Pray

What does it mean to you knowing that Christ died on the cross for you?

Humbles me!

If you know Christ as your Savior, it's exciting to read these words and think about what it was like when you first felt God place His call of salvation on your life?

DAY 2

Leaning In: Giving God Control

"Trust in the Lord with all your heart and lean not on your own understanding; in all your ways acknowledge him and he will make your paths straight." PROVERBS 3:5 & 6 NIV

Before we can step into drawing closer to God, we must be willing to give control over to God. We must believe that His Word and promises are true. And in order to hand over the control, we have to trust Him. This is a very basic concept, but it can be hard to put into practice.

Today we are looking at Proverbs 3:5&6. These are very familiar verses that begin, *"Trust in the Lord with ALL your heart..."*

Life throws us curves and trusting can be very hard. We have all been hurt by people we thought we could trust or have been faced with an unexpected circumstance that brings our world crashing in around us.

But the Lord can always be trusted. He created us and loves us and knows each of us better than we know ourselves. We can trust in the Lord with all our heart.

Next, the verse says, "*...lean not on your own understanding; in all your ways acknowledge him.*" We will not always understand everything going on in our life at that moment, but if we trust in the Lord and hold tight to His Word, which is filled with His promises, and if we lean on that understanding, giving Him praise and acknowledging His presence in the midst of whatever situation is going on. Then there is a promise at the end of the verse, that says, "*...he shall make your paths straight.*"

Now does that mean all hardships just fall away and the roads are perfectly smooth? No! By trusting Him, leaning in and acknowledging Him, our perspective changes. "Leaning in" is a term I coined from the difficulties I faced while training for a mini marathon. When the wind is brisk, or the road is steep, you must learn to "lean in" to counter their effects. Every time I found myself "leaning in" I would think, this is how I need to be with God. When the brisk winds and steep hills of life come against us, we need to "lean in" to HIM! When we do, we shift control from ourselves to Him, our precious Lord, who wants to guide us over the rough roads of life.

Instead of rushing head long into whatever you are facing. You ought to "lean in" and trust Jesus because "*...he will make your paths straight.*"

Pause, Ponder and Pray

Imagine yourself "leaning in" to the arms of your heavenly Father, and ask yourself:

In what areas do I need to give God control over?

Why is it so hard for me to let God have control?

What are some steps I can take that will help me trust God and give control over to Him?

1. Put His will first!
2. Follow when He urges me onward to do something!

DAY 3

Breaking Free

"The thief comes only to steal and kill and destroy; I have come that they may have life, and have it to the full." JOHN 10:10 NIV

First, we need to know that these are red letter words in the Bible, which mean they are words that Jesus spoke! Jesus was sharing a parable about eternal life and how the shepherd takes care of his sheep, but the purpose of the thief is to kill, steal and destroy.

On page 1636 in the Moody Bible Commentary, it says that the thief does not just refer to Satan, but to any false teachers. I would go as far as to say a thief is anyone, or anything, that causes you to stumble and not live up to your full potential. A thief is not worried about taking care of the sheep, a thief only wants whatever they can get for themselves.

An example of how the thief kills, steals and destroys is by continually parading your past shortcomings through your mind. We all have things in our past that cause us to pull back, keeping us from sharing the gospel and causes us to not step up and live life in the fullness that Christ has for us because we don't feel worthy.

I allowed being 16 and pregnant, then married and divorced, to hold me back. I felt I had multiple scarlet letters that everyone knew about, there were times when I would allow the guilt that came from knowing sex outside of marriage was not God's plan, and I perceived being divorced as a double dose of disappointment. Basically, I allowed the thief to steal, kill and destroy my identity.

To look at my life now some 20 plus years later, my life is more stable because I no longer allow my past to define my identity.

Think about this, "We assume that everyone knows our past, but we never assume that people know we are redeemed!" And here's something to ponder, "Do we allow ourselves to live like we have been redeemed and that we are forgiven?"

What I learned was that I needed to turn my thinking around and stop listening to the thief because of what Christ Jesus did on the cross. If we believe and accept Jesus as our risen Savior, HE has broken the bond that our past had over us. Are we living that way?

Notice it was Jesus's work on the cross that set us free and we just need to accept His gift to live in His freedom. Whenever our past raises its ugly head, we need to put it back into its place by taking those thoughts captive and holding them to the light of scripture. One way I did this was by getting up every morning and looking at myself in the mirror, telling myself that God loved me so much that He sent His Son to shed His blood for me. And asking myself, "Am I living like I'm loved that much?"

Jesus says in John 15:13, *"Greater love has no one than this, that he lay down his life for his friends."* Jesus is my friend who dearly loves me!

I'm not going to lie, this was not just a onetime thing and done, this was every morning, and sometimes multiple times throughout the day, until I started to accept that my worth was found in Jesus, not in my past, not in the lies the thief kept whispering in my ear.

Our past should serve us, not define us.

Pause, Ponder and Pray

Are there situations from your past that still has a hold on you?

Do you believe that Jesus set you free from bondage?

What are some steps you can put into place so that when the past raises its ugly head, you can put it back in its place?

DAY 4

Pressing Toward the Goal

"Brothers, I do not consider myself yet to have taken hold of it. But one thing I do: Forgetting what is behind and straining toward what is ahead." PHILIPPIANS 3:13 NIV

This verse holds a very dear place in my heart because it helped me to extend forgiveness to others after I became a Christian. There was as time I was so angry, that all it did was consume me. I was still a babe in my faith and a very wise person shared this verse with me. They asked me, "Can you see yourself forgetting what is behind you and straining forward, like a runner in a relay, to what is ahead for you?" Honestly at that point in my walk, I could not. But what I did do was this, I would pray, "Lord you know how I feel. I'm not even sure what forgiveness really looks like in my situation, but my heart hurts and I'm tired of it hurting like it does. Help me to forget the past and strain forward to what is ahead." Then I would read and reread this passage. I don't remember now how long I continued to do this, but it was for a few months. I do remember one night as I opened my Bible to read and pray, as I read this passage, I realized all those angry emotions that I usually felt were gone. I don't know exactly when the Lord changed my heart, but He did.

Remember this verse says, "*...Forgetting what is behind....*", I don't believe you ever forget your past as it is part of you. As we learned yesterday, the thief wants to use your past against you, but our past no longer has the hold on us it once did. Just as my situation used to spark intense feelings of anger, by the grace of God, it no longer has a hold on me. Like Paul understood, it's a process that we should be continually striving towards that which Christ has called us.

Pause, Ponder and Pray

What do you need to put behind you?

What do you need to be reaching for? (Hint a good goal is found in verse 14)

DAY 5

Do the Work

"David also said to Solomon his son, "Be Strong and courageous, and do the work. Do not be afraid or discouraged, for the Lord, God, my God is with you. He will not fail you or forsake you until all the work for the service of the temple of the Lord is finished."

1 CHRONICLES 28:20 NIV

For over a year, the Lord continually laid Joshua 1:9 on my heart, *"Have I not commanded you? Be strong and courageous. Do not be terrified; do not be discouraged, for the Lord your God will be with you wherever you go."* And as you can see, today's verse in 1 Chronicles is similar to the verse in Joshua. David was passing the torch, so to speak to his son Solomon. David was giving Solomon instructions on building the temple, encouraging him for the task, but David included three little words, *"...do the work..."*.

After spending a year learning to be stronger and more courageous, "do the work" had a huge impact on my life. I realized The Lord has work for all of us to do, and just as Joshua and Solomon needed to be reminded, we too need be reminded to be strong and courageous and then *"do the work"*.

You might be saying, I don't know what work I'm to do? Your work will depend on where you are in your walk with the Lord. The work for some might be that of getting into the discipline of seeking God and being in His Word more consistently. For me, *"do the work"* has been the time, miles and tears that have gone into these 21 devotions. This has been much harder than I anticipated, and I had to hold on to the end of this verse to get me through. "*He* [the Lord] *will not fail you or forsake you until all the work for the service of the temple of the Lord is finished."* There were days I wanted to quit, telling myself, "Writing is not my thing."

At one time, I was like, "Lord, you realize I'm not building a temple, right?

"No, you're building a legacy, MY legacy, do the work."

"Um, I'm running out of time and writing is hard, I'm facing a deadline, you know."

"Trust me"

Please understand I do not mean to be flippant with my Lord. However, I lay it right out there. I talk with God like I would be talking with you right now, after all, God knows you better than you know yourself. Most the time, God doesn't need to hear your words, you need to hear your words to be able to make a change.

The Lord kept reinforcing be strong and courageous. Moses was dead, and Joshua was now leading the people. Sometimes God asks us to step up and step out. It can be scary. But just as in Joshua 1, the Lord isn't going to ask you to do something and then step away from you. As the Lords says in Joshua 1:5, *"...As I was with Moses, so I will be with you; I will never leave you nor forsake you."*

As I've learned, *"until all the work for the service of the temple of the Lord is finished,"* simply means for that particular assignment. "Do the work" is going to be a continual call!

Pause, Ponder and Pray

Allow God to make you strong and courageous, then "do the work!"

What "work" is God calling you to?

DAY 6

Growing and Stretching

"Consider it pure joy, my brothers and sisters, whenever you face trials of any kind, because you know the testing of your faith produces perseverance. Let perseverance finish its work so that you may be mature and complete, not lacking anything." James 1:2-4 NIV

Growing, it sounds like a great concept, we all want to grow until we realize that often pain is involved. Why is there pain involved? Because we are being stretched and molded into Christlikeness. I always laugh at this because I have a few memorable moments where God really stretched me outside of my comfort zone. One of the most memorable was when I was asked to serve on a team for a youth weekend retreat. I served because I was asked, and it sounded like fun. But as the weekend went on I realized God was stretching me WAY outside of my comfort zone. On the first day of the retreat I remember walking to the front of the chapel with the other pastors, thinking, "What in the world am I doing here? I am not a pastor, I'm in WAY over my head, God you got the wrong person!"

Now, I can look back and chuckle, I mean, have you ever told God He had the wrong person? God does have a BIG sense of humor. And with hindsight being 20/20, I can now see God was showing me where He wanted to take me if I would allow Him, making my experience a positive one.

It's easier to see God in those hard moments when we have trained ourselves to see Him. When we have learned to "lean in" to Him. As I've learned, we grow most in the valleys, because in the valley you are forced to either rely on God or walk away from God. Since this lesson is on growing closer to God, I'm going to assume we all are "leaning in" to God during our darkest days, saying, "Show me Lord! Grow me Lord!"

Because I've allowed God to stretch me and learn from the experiences, what hurt so bad a few years ago, is now a more comfortable place for me to be.

What happens when what you're facing is hard or down right hurts your heart. Are you still to consider it pure joy?

Of course, God is using those heartbreaking moments to grow us and draw us closer to him. "*Let perseverance finish its work so that you may be mature and complete, not lacking anything.*"

Pause, Ponder and Pray

What is your "consider it pure joy" moment?

What do you think God was growing in you during that time?

DAY 7

Rely on God

"And so we know and rely on the love God has for us. God is love. Whoever lives in love lives in God, and God in him." 1 JOHN 4:16 NIV

This was the verse at The Living Stone church for 2017, and the theme was love. For some reason, I could never get excited about this verse. All I heard when I read this verse was love, love, love and it might as well have been, blah, blah, blah. I was still stuck on our verse from 2016, which was Ephesians 3:20, *"Now to him who is able to do immeasurably more than we ask or imagine, according to his power that is at work within us,"* now that verse got me excited! I think it was because this verse challenged me to step out and trust God more, knowing that God was able to do immeasurably more than I could ever ask or imagine because it was His power that was at work within me.

After 8 months of reading this verse in 1 John, it finally clicked. I had only been focusing on the love part of this verse, because that was the church's theme for the year. But the Spirit spoke to my heart and said what I needed to be focusing on first was the part about relying on God.

For those who know me, you know that I'm a very driven person and I forget that I'm not a one woman show. Sometimes I get ahead of God, and when I do, I'm not relying on Him at ALL. It more like I'm saying, "Hey, God I'm going to do x-y-z". And God probably shakes His head and wonders when is she ever going to learn.

I looked up "rely" in the Merriam-Webster's Dictionary, which says 1. *To be dependent* 2. *To have confidence based on experience*. When I thought about these definitions, Ephesians 3:20 and our verse for the year then it became exciting for me. Because I could rely on God, I had confidence in Him, based on my experiences through Him, allowing Him to do immeasurably more than I could ask or imagine.

When you rely on God, by the power of the Holy Spirit, then love is the by-product. Why? Because "... *God is love.*" It really is as simple as resting and relying on God.

Rely on God and live in His love as God lives in you!!!!

Pause, Ponder and Pray

What keeps you from fully relying on God?

How do "you" live in God's love?

What is one thing that God has done in your life that was immeasurably more than you could have imagined?

DAY 8

Wholeheartedly

"He did what was right in the eyes of the Lord, but not wholeheartedly."
2 CHRONICLES 25:2 NIV

This verse summarizes King Amaziah trying to live a godly life. He did what was right, but not with all his heart. When you hear the word wholehearted, what do you think of? When I hear the word wholehearted I think of a person who has great passion or zeal. They just can't help but to get "into" whatever they are doing.

This is what the Moody Bible Commentary has this to say about being wholehearted, "*to have a whole heart would mean a "steadfast heart", an "up right heart", an "obedient heart", and a "devoted to God heart". In effect King Amaziah's reign was a mixture of listening to and submitting to the Word of God or the word of a prophet, but also filled with rash decisions and self-serving pride. (pg 619)*"

I had to include that last sentence because I know I can see myself in it. OUCH! Sometimes I can be rash, sometimes I can be filled with self-serving pride. BUT, unlike King Amaziah, my story isn't finished yet and being rash and self-serving is not how I want to be known.

So how do we change that? For me personally, when I started looking at my life and asking myself, "Where is Jesus in this situation?" and then started thanking and praising Him for all he has done in my life, my passion went deeper and I started seeing the opportunities I had to serve Him and others, that is when I started to be wholehearted! Knowing that wholeheartedness is a process.

And then I just allow myself to be blown away by the idea that, God does not need me at all, for anything. Yet He wants to use me, even all the messed-up parts of me! Knowing that it's Him in me, makes me want to live a life of wholehearted devotion, one that hopefully others will see and wonder, "What does she have that I don't?" with the obvious answer being, Jesus!!!!

This reminded me of John 4:13 & 14 when Jesus told the woman at the well, "*Everyone who drinks this water will be thirsty again, but whoever drinks the water I give him will never thirst. Indeed, the water I give him will become in him a spring of water welling up to eternal life.*"

Who doesn't want to drink deep from the living waters our Lord Jesus and live wholeheartedly?

Pause, Ponder and Pray

What might wholeheartedness look like in you?

What are some steps you can implement to help you to start living wholeheartedly in the eyes of the Lord?

DAY 9

Training

"Everyone who competes in the games goes into strict training. They do it to get a crown that will not last, but we do it to get a crown that will last forever." 1 CORINTHIANS 9:25 NIV

Do you remember as kids the discipline that was required to play sports? I remember in high school all the running we did for Basketball. I hated running. I only did it because I had a coach pushing/yelling at me to do it. As you dig into the meaning of this verse, you find that YOU must be the coach and put yourself into strict training.

For an athlete, it is nothing for them to spend several hours a day training, but can you see yourself spending HOURS studying the Word of God? That might sound crazy at first but let me share part of my journey. When I first realized that I needed to spend more time reading my Bible, I had a baby and a 2 yr old at home. My time was precious. I felt I didn't have a minute to spare, so I decided to get up 15 minutes earlier every morning and read. As I read and then started journaling, I found 15 minutes just wasn't enough time, so I got up 30 minutes earlier than I had before. After a few months I was surprised to find that 30 minutes flew by and I wasn't ready to stop, so I started getting up an hour before everyone else. I knew I needed to start my day being grounded and established in God's Word in order to face the struggles and trials that each day would bring.

Yes, there were days I was tired, days I did not want to get up, days that it was hard, but I did it anyway. Thankfully as soon as I got into the Word, I would forget about being tired or wanting to sleep, or whatever else might had been trying to keep me from my "training." I was blessed beyond measure by giving that time to God.

In my "training time" God was feeding me. He caused a hunger in me for His Word that drove me to get up early. This reminds me of Deuteronomy 8:3 that says, *"He humbled you, causing you to hunger and then feeding you with manna, which neither you nor your fathers had known, to teach you that man does not live by bread alone but on every word that comes from the mouth of the Lord."*

In this passage Moses was reminding the people what the Lord had done for them as they wandered in the wilderness for 40 years . God was training his people to rely on him. He caused them to have a need that only he could meet. I saw that he was doing the same for me in the time I spent with Him each morning.

When you have trained long enough, it becomes a part of you, it's a lifestyle. It is trustworthy. A friend told me once, "Trust your study" she could have said, "Trust your training!"

Pause, Ponder and Pray

As a Christian, do you see the need for strict training in God's Word?

How much time do you spend DAILY studying God's word? Are you happy with that amount of time?

Do you feel like God might be asking more of you? Are you willing to get up earlier to spend more time in His Word?

DAY 10

Your Healer

---

[43] And a woman was there who had been subject to bleeding for twelve years, but no one could heal her. [44] She came up behind him and touched the edge of his cloak, and immediately her bleeding stopped.

[45] "Who touched me?" Jesus asked.

When they all denied it, Peter said, "Master, the people are crowding and pressing against you."

[46] But Jesus said, "Someone touched me; I know that power has gone out from me."

[47] Then the woman, seeing that she could not go unnoticed, came trembling and fell at his feet. In the presence of all the people, she told why she had touched him and how she had been instantly healed. [48] Then he said to her, "Daughter, your faith has healed you. Go in peace." LUKE 8:43-48 NIV

This woman's determination fascinates me, her story is found in 3 of the 4 gospels. Matthew only gives 2 verses to the event, but Mark and Luke go into much greater detail.

We get the picture that there were many people there, as Peter said, *"Master, the people are crowding and pressing against you."* But in Luke 8:42 it said, *"...the crowds almost crushed him..."*

Almost crushed him? Can you imagine what this crowd must have really been like, it was more than just pressing on him, it was crushing Him, showing us how badly this woman must have wanted to just get close to Jesus. She was probably weak from bleeding for 12 years. She was considered unclean and a social outcast. The scene was so chaotic the people in the crowd must not have even realized she was there, or they would have moved away from her, because by coming in contact with her they would have become unclean too.

Everything was against her. But she wanted to encounter Jesus so badly NOTHING was going to hold her back. This woman knew in her heart of hearts this man they called the Messiah would heal her. How did she know this? By faith!

Jesus said to her daughter your faith has healed you. Hebrews 11:1 defines faith for us. *"Now faith is being sure of what we hope for and certain of what we do not see."* By faith, long before she had her encounter with Jesus, she was certain that if she could just touch the hem of His garment she would be healed. Her determination is what drove her to push through the crowd and get to Jesus.

Is your faith determined by certainty? By faith we too can seek Jesus's healing. For me, I had to redefine healing. I used to think of healing just as described in this verse. An instant touch from the Lord and instantly healed. While miraculous healing still takes place, often it is a process that takes time, both of which require faith.

Pause, Ponder and Pray

Can you imagine what would it have been like to *be* the woman in the crowd?

What is keeping you from pushing through and touching Jesus?

Have faith that Jesus still heals! He still does miracles!

DAY 11

Making Better Choices

"This is what the Lord says:

"Stand at the crossroads and look; ask for the ancient paths, and where the good way is, and walk in it, and you will find rest for your souls. But you said, 'We will not walk in it.'" JEREMIAH 6:16 NIV

As I was reading the book, *21 Days of Prayer for your Business*, Jeremiah 6:16 was the verse for Day 5, and it made a lasting impression on me. I think it's because the older I get, the more I realize that God's ancient ways are the best ways. Daily we stand at crossroads with a choice to make between the right paths and the wrong paths. Hopefully, if it's between an obvious right and wrong path, the choice is easy. But there are times when we must choose between two good paths, and that can be harder.

When I'm faced with that type of decision, I spend LOTS of time praying and seeking God for clarity, which means spending lots of time being in HIS word. I've found that being in God's Word and seeking His guidance for my life does not happen by accident. Simply put, we must be intentional in seeking God for guidance and direction in choosing the better path. So, here's a question to think about, how much of the time that you spend seeking God for guidance, is done intentionally to find what He knows is best for your life? Ouch!

We tend to do things rashly and without thinking. But God says to, *"Stand at the crossroads and look,"* the "look" means to stop and ponder; to pause, contemplate, and observe so that you are able to make the better choice. The reason He says this is because His ways are not our ways, as Isaiah 55:8-9 says, *"For my thoughts are not your thoughts, neither are your ways my ways," declares the Lord. "As the heavens are higher than the earth, so are my ways higher than your ways and my thoughts higher than your thoughts."* It's in the time of looking and praying that we find the better path.

Remember we were told to stand at the crossroads and ask for the ancient path, "*where the good way is, and* then *walk in it, to find rest for our souls*". Who doesn't want that? That's our goal!

Unfortunately, our verse finishes with, *"We will not walk in it."* Proving that people have been thick-headed for a long time. If you make the best choice as a result of seeking God, you will find rest for your soul, or you can continue doing your own thing. The choice is yours.

Pause, Ponder and Pray

Are you intentionally seeking God for His ancient ways?

Or, do you find yourself in the, "*I will not walk in it*" kind of attitude?

DAY 12

Gifts Are Meant to Be Shared

"It was he who gave some to be apostles, some to be prophets, some to be evangelists, and some to be pastors and teachers, to prepare God's people for works of service, so that the body of Christ may be built up..." EPHESIANS 4:11 & 12 NIV

How many times have you said, "I just don't know what my gifts are." Multiple times in the Bible we read about gifts being given and then using those gifts for God's purpose, yet we become frustrated because we don't seem to know what our gifts are.

I like lists. Both Romans 12:6-8, and 1 Corinthians 12:7-10, 28-30 lists many spiritual gifts, but these do not include every spiritual gift. As a young Christian I would read these lists never really seeing myself in any of them. It was frustrating. I was good with horses, but I never found any place in the Bible that said, "Good with Horses" was a spiritual gift. What I came to realize was that many of the things I learned from the horse's, God grew into a spiritual gift that I do my best to use to bring Him glory and honor.

See we can't all be preachers or teachers or administrators, or whatever gift you might find more important than the gifts God has given you. That is why 1 Peter 4:10 says, *"Each one should use whatever gift he has received to serve others, faithfully administering God's grace in its various forms."*

We are all called to serve, and by doing so we are living examples of God's grace and mercy for everyone! How cool is that! I hope this challenges you to step out and serve in area that you are NOT comfortable in. Yes, you heard me right, do what seems uncomfortable! God has many opportunities waiting to use your spiritual gifts, even the ones you didn't know you had.

For me, God is using this 21 Day Challenge to show me a gift I didn't know He wanted me to use. This style of writing is not my passion, but I do enjoy being in God's Word, sharing what I've learned, and seeing what that looks like in my life because if I'm willing to share my struggles and how God works in me, maybe it will help someone else draw closer to Him.

The point I want you to take from today's Challenge, is that your gift is not for you. It is for the building up of the body of Christ, one body, many parts.

Pause, Ponder and Pray

Are you doing your part by plugging yourself into your church or other areas of ministries to see the gift you weren't even aware of that God wants to grow to maturity?

Are you willing to serve in those areas, to trust God to grow a new skill in you?

DAY 13

Narrow Your Focus

"Enter through the narrow gate. For wide is the gate and broad is the road that leads to destruction, and many enter through it."
MATTHEW 7:13 NIV

We've all heard someone say, "Everyone's doing it." You might have even said those words to your parents or maybe your grandparents at some time in your life and they probably responded to you with, "Well, you're not everyone and if everyone jumped off a bridge. Would you?" That little dialog reminds me of this verse in Matthew where Jesus is trying to teach that "The Way" is through the narrow gate.

This lesson teaches me 3 things.

First, **I can't be afraid to walk with Christ, apart from the world**: We are told in Matthew to *enter through the narrow gate,* but not everyone is going to find or even look for the narrow gate. In John 10:9 Jesus says, *"I am the gate; whoever enters through me will be saved. He will come in and go out, and find pasture."*

Second, **I need to enter**: Jesus is the gate, and I need to be the one intentionally entering through Him. This verse says, *"Wide is the gate and broad the road that leads to destruction, and many enter through it."* Wide and broad means to me, that many can fit on that road and the resistance is minimal, but our human nature tends to lead us along the path of least resistance! Now I'm not saying that if it is easy it is bad. I'm just saying that Jesus says to enter through the narrow gate, and for me that means seeking Him wholeheartedly. When life seems to be going easy, it is wise to check yourself against scripture to make sure you are still on the narrow road.

Third, **It's probably not going to be easy**: Jeremiah 29:13 says, *"You will seek me and find me when you seek me with all your heart."* Seeking Jesus intentionally and wholeheartedly takes effort. Finding the narrow road isn't always easy to see, and it is imperative that we have a close personal relationship with Jesus. You develop that kind of relationship by being in His word regularly. Not just reading short devotionals like this one but using them as a springboard to go deeper into the word of God. It's good to read portions of Bible, but to gain perspective you need to read ALL of it, from beginning to end, realizing you won't completely understand it the first time you read it! However, in reading ALL of the Bible you will find familiar passages or verses that speak meaning, comfort and understanding into your life.

This is why I said, "It's probably not going to be easy." But when you seek Jesus wholeheartedly, you will find Him!

Pause, Ponder and Pray

Are we afraid to walk apart from the world?

What do you need to do to be more intentional?

When life is hard, what sustains you? Do you have a special verse to cling to when the wide road looks appealing?

If so, write it down. If not, ask the Lord to lead you to one, and then write it down.

DAY 14

Clothe Yourselves

"Therefore, as God's chosen people, holy and dearly loved, clothe yourselves with compassion, kindness, humility, gentleness and patience. Bear with each other and forgive whatever grievances you may have against one another. Forgive as the Lord forgave you. And over all these virtues put on love which binds them all together in perfect unity." COLOSSIANS 3:12-14 NIV

I love this verse because it establishes my identity. Who am I? I am one of God's chosen people. I am holy and dearly loved, just as you are. This reminds me of 1 Peter 1:15 & 16 that says, "*But just as he who called you is holy, so be holy in all you do; for it is written: "Be holy, because I am holy."*" But what is holy? I looked up "holy" in the Merriam-Webster's Dictionary and the 4th definition was most fitting for this context. It says, "Having a divine quality." So, I have a divine quality because of the Holy Spirit within me as I am one of God's chosen!

The verse goes on to says clothe yourselves with compassion, kindness, humility, gentleness and patience, reminding me of the fruit of the Spirit found in Galatians 5:22-23, "*But the fruit of the Spirit is love, joy, peace, forbearance, kindness, goodness, faithfulness, gentleness and self-control. Against such things there is no law.*" So, I have the ability to "clothe" myself with Christlikeness because of the power of the Holy Spirit in me, by doing that, these traits should be evident in my life. When I was younger, I had a very quick and explosive temper. I still have a temper, but the fuse is much longer now, and that is only by the grace of God. It is only by realizing that I'm a daughter of the King, chosen and dearly loved, that I don't have to allow my emotions to get the best of me. I can clothe myself with Christlike attributes by putting into practice Romans 12:2a, "*Do not conform to the pattern of this world, but be transformed by the renewing of your mind...*"

The verses in Colossians goes on to says, "*bear with each other and forgive whatever grievances you may have against one another.*" While this is not easy, the word "bear" brings to mind the word endure. Sometimes we need to endure people and their not-so-Christlike attitudes as they do ours. We are usually quick to see worldly ways in others but never in ourselves! Ouch! But Praise God there is hope! We are told to "*forgive as the Lord forgave you*"*!* While this is a tall order it can be accomplished through love. We are to "*put on love which bind them all together in perfect unity*". Love is the glue that holds all these traits together. If we clothe ourselves with love, then even our differences can become positives, bringing us together in unity. You can practice compassion, kindness, humility, gentleness and patience, but without love, what is the reason behind them? Love is our motivator for Christlikeness. Why? Because God is Love. The Love of God is what makes us holy!

Loving our brothers and sisters is a choice we make, not a feeling we have.

Pause, Ponder and Pray

What are some of the Christlike traits you see in yourself, and ones that need improving?

Do you consciously clothe yourself with Christlikeness?

See yourself putting on these Christlike traits and discarding other worldly traits.

DAY 15

Worship 24/7/365

"Therefore, I urge you, brothers, in view of God's mercy, to offer your bodies as living sacrifices, holy and pleasing to God- this is our spiritual worship. Do not conform any longer to the pattern of this world but be transformed by the renewing of your mind. Then you will be able to test and approve what God's will is-his good, pleasing and perfect will." ROMANS 12:1-2 NIV

Much of the time when we hear the word worship we think it only has to do with praise music. I'm not saying that music doesn't play an important part in worship, many times God will put a song on my heart that fills me with joy and just flows out of me. Trust me it's a joyful noise, not a beautiful noise, but God loves it anyway! One song that really gets me excited about worship is Chris Tomlin's, "Lay Me Down." I get excited because it reminds me what true worship is all about. The song talks of the joy that is found when we lay down our life and wholly give it to the Lord! I highly recommend you Google this song and listen to it.

We don't think enough about making our lives living sacrifices, but we should as this is, *"holy and pleasing to God!*" When we lay down our lives, and by that, I mean all those things that we place over God, like my attitude, my desires; whatever it may be that I selfishly want. But when we come to the point to lay it ALL down, then we are beginning to put God's will ahead of ours. That's sacrificial worship!

David gave us an example of this in 2 Samuel 6:14, "*David, wearing a linen ephod, danced before the Lord with all his might.*" David put his whole being into his act of worship unconcerned of how he looked to others! You could say he was on fire for God! However, David's wife was not impressed. In fact, she was mortified at his behavior, thinking he looked foolish! But David didn't care because when you come to a place of allowing the Spirit to fill you and flow out of you, then worship becomes a 24/7/365 thing! People might not understand where your joy is coming from. Some will even try to rain on your parade, but don't let them as this is a time to draw even closer to the Lord!

Psalm 100 gives us a beautiful picture of the Lord and why we can worship him wholeheartedly!

Psalm 100

1 Shout for joy to the LORD, all the earth.
2 Worship the LORD with gladness;
come before him with joyful songs.
3 Know that the LORD is God.

It is he who made us, and we are his;
we are his people, the sheep of his pasture.
4 Enter his gates with thanksgiving
and his courts with praise;
give thanks to him and praise his name.
5 For the LORD is good and his love endures forever;
his faithfulness continues through all generations.

Sacrificial worship takes effort, but praising God 24/7/365 will change your life.

Pause, Ponder and Pray

Do you want to experience uninhibited worship?

Can you see yourself, like David, worshiping the Lord unashamed and unconcerned of what others might think?

If so, allow the Spirit to lead you in wholehearted worship by not conforming to the opinions of the world, but being transformed by the renewing of your mind.

DAY 16

The Example Set for Us

"Be imitators of God, therefore, as dearly loved children, and live a life of love, just as Christ loved us and gave himself up for us as a fragrant offering and sacrifice to God." EPHESIANS 5:1-2 NIV

In 1 Corinthians 11:1 Paul tells us, "*Follow my example, as I follow the example of Christ.*" We tend to read the Bible and then forget that what we just read really does apply to us today. I want to hit on just a few of the obvious ways that Jesus is our example.

Frist, loving others. Today's verse hits on this topic. Jesus loves each of us so much that He gave himself up for us, for you and for me. This is a deep sacrificial love, and even though we have the example, how much do we love like that? In John 13:34-35, Jesus commands us to love. "*A new command I give to you: Love one another. As I have loved you, so you must love one another. By this all men will know you are my disciples.*" Loving like Jesus sets us apart so that others know that we are disciples of Christ.

Jesus taught us about humbly serving others. In John 13:12-15, "*When he finished washing their feet he put on his clothes and returned to his place. "Do you understand what I have done for you?" he asked them. "You call me 'Teacher' and 'Lord,' and rightly so, for that is what I am. Now that I, your Lord and Teacher, have washed your feet, you should also wash one another's feet. I have set an example that you should do as I have done for you. I tell you the truth, no servant is greater than his master, nor is a messenger greater than the one who sent him. Now that you know these things, you will be blessed if you do them."* The disciples didn't understand all that was taking place, but Jesus very clearly told them that He had set an example for them and that they should do as He had done. And since they had seen His example, they would be blessed if they followed Him.

Jesus taught us to pray. There are many examples of Jesus praying and in Matthew 6:9-13 Jesus is specifically teaching on prayer. This passage is known as the Lord's Prayer, *"This, then, is how you should pray: "'Our Father in heaven, hallowed be your name, your kingdom come, your will be done, on earth as it is in heaven. Give us today our daily bread. And forgive us our debts, as we also have forgiven our debtors. And lead us not into temptation, but deliver us from the evil one.'* The Lord's Prayer is an outline on how to pray. Giving glory and honor to the Lord, acknowledging His power, asking for provision and protection, knowing that the Lord will give according to His will, not ours. Seeing our need for forgiveness and knowing we are to forgive others and knowing that everything comes from the very hand of God.

We also learn about forgiveness, in Luke 23:34 Jesus says, "*Father, forgive them for they do not know what they are doing.*" This was Jesus practicing what He had preached when He walked this earth. He taught it and then lived it. As Jesus hung on the cross, He asked His Father to forgive the men that hung Him there. What is the example for us? We have all had people hurt us, but did you ever consider that they did not know what they were doing? Even if they did, we are called to forgive them as we have been forgiven

Jesus taught us about submission and obedience as well. It is my opinion that you can't be completely obedient without submission. In John 6:38 Jesus says, "*For I have come down from heaven not to do my will but to do the will of him who sent me.*" Jesus was perfect in His obedience to His Father because He was submitted to the will of the Father before He was ever sent to earth. I truthfully never gave the submission part much thought till one year for Lent our Pastor asked us what we were going to give up. Now In my quiet time that week I asked the Lord, not really expecting an answer, "What am I supposed to give up?" As quick as I asked, I heard the words in my mind, "Your will." That was a deer in the headlight moment for me. It was a clear moment of knowing that God had just called me out. I could attempt obedience, but without being submissive, my strong will was hindrance to my obedience. For our obedience to bring glory to God, our will has to be surrendered to His. Now this was not an immediate surrendering of all my will, it is something I must continually do, but the more I surrendered to God's will the easier it is to be obedient to Him.

These are just a few of the examples that Jesus gave us, but I honestly believe there is an answer in the Bible for anything you might face. The Bible isn't a Magic 8 Ball that you shake and say, "Ok Jesus what is the answer?" It's spending the time building your relationship with Him and seeking His example.

Pause, Ponder and Pray

What situation do you need God to show you an example for?

Train yourself to seek Jesus's example in all things!

DAY 17

Servant Leadership

"For we are God's workmanship created in Christ Jesus to do good works, which God prepared in advance for us to do."
EPHESIANS 2:10 NIV

Often, we only see our shortcomings, but have you ever wondered that if they were grown or pruned a bit that they might actually bring glory to God? Now, I'm not pointing fingers, (If I did, I would have to point them all at me.) But one such trait I was thinking of is bossiness. No one likes someone who is bossy, yet if that trait is pruned, groomed and grown, then a bossy person could become a great leader. Better yet a servant leader, a *workman created in Christ Jesus to do good works.*

In Mark 10:35-45, James and John came to the Lord and asked if they could sit at each side of Jesus. Jesus told them they did not know what they were asking because they did not understand the idea of servant leadership, yet. (Everyone still thought Jesus would overthrow the government and they would be taking a physical presence in this world.) Jesus says to them in verse 43, *"Not so with you. Instead whoever wants to become great among you must be your servant, and whoever wants to be first must be a slave of all."* Another note about this passage is that James and John were also known as the Sons of Thunder, giving me the picture of someone who is still being pruned, groomed and grown, and might tend to be rash and aggressive yet very passionate in what they do! I can relate to them a great deal as I tend to be rash, aggressive and very passionate, but praise be to God, by the power of the Holy Spirit and allowing His pruning, grooming and growing we can learn servant leadership!

I saw an example of this at a church fellowship meal. I saw our Pastor roll up his sleeves and help serve the people of his congregation. I don't know if anyone else even noticed, but I thought, "There is a picture of servant leadership in action." Most people probably didn't even think twice about him filling cups, carrying plates, or just doing whatever needed to be done. And he did this until everyone had been served. Of course, our Pastor wasn't the only one helping to serve, but I just loved the image of "rolling up our sleeves" in order to serve others.

We are God's workmanship when we put on Christlikeness and get busy being servant leaders. This is essentially saying we are ready to step into the work that *God has prepared in advance for us to do!* Roll up your sleeves and serve!

Pause, Ponder and Pray

What traits do you have that need to be pruned, groomed and grown to make you a better servant leader? i.e. self-righteousness, pride, your will

Are you ready to step into the work that God prepared in advance for you to do?

DAY 18

Life isn't a Sprint

"I have fought the good fight, I have finished the race. I have kept the faith." 2 TIMOTHY 4:7 NIV

We live such busy lives. It is hurry here and hurry there. Jumping from one thing to the next. Not really taking the time to settle into the race the Lord has for us.

These words from Paul wrap up his life. His time on the earth is short and he is passing on a last bit of wisdom to Timothy and ultimately to us. In this verse Paul says, "*I have fought the good fight.*" These words strike in me the image of a fight that has been long and drawn out, losing some of the rounds, but never giving up, he kept on going till the very end.

A look back over Paul's life, he was first known as Saul and one of the greatest persecutors of early Christians. Then he had a life changing encounter with the living God and then the Lord gave him the name Paul. Paul then went on to preach the gospel near and far. Winding up in prison, beaten numerous times and ultimately sentenced to death, being beheaded for his faith. Yet, he considered his death as gain. Even while imprisoned Paul preached the gospel to the Romans who guarded him. Paul never stopped running the race assigned to him. It was the course the Lord had laid out for him and so Paul could say with great certainty, *"I have kept the faith."*

As I was training for a mini marathon, I would break up my training into walk/run sections. I would run for a mile or 2 and then walk a mile to recover my energy for the next run section. I found that if I started running again too fast, working too hard, I was going to wear out. I had to learn to run continually. I wouldn't stop, I would just slow down, concentrate on my stride, focus on my breathing and hitting a slower pace so that it wasn't as taxing on my body,

You can train yourself to run and finish the race or you can make life so busy by running hard and wearing yourself out. Life isn't to be lived to just die, it's to cross the finish line and being able to say, like Paul, *"I have fought the good fight, I have finished the race, I have kept the faith."*

Pause, Ponder and Pray

Life isn't a sprint! Is being too busy making it hard to run the race the Lord has for you?

Life isn't to be lived to just die, it is to finish well.

DAY 19

Living and Active

"For the word of God is living and active. Sharper than any double-edged sword, it penetrates even to dividing soul and spirit, joints and marrow; it judges the thoughts and attitudes of the heart."

HEBREWS 4:12 NIV

God has been speaking to His people through His Word for years and that is how He still speaks to His people today. As we draw closer to Day 21 of this Devotional, I hope you have seen the benefit of putting your own "work" into getting to know the Lord in a more personal way. You have done that by being in His Word but imagine being in all of it!

Don't just take my word for it, continue to taste the Word of God for yourself each day. He will prove His faithfulness to you in seeking Him wholeheartedly.

In 1 Samuel, when Samuel was a child studying under Eli chapter 3:1 says, *"...In those days the word of the Lord was rare;"*. Part of the reason for this was that there were not many who were even seeking God, much less looking to have a close personal relationship with Him. In verse 7 we see that the Lord called out to Samuel, but Samuel didn't recognize His voice. *"Now Samuel did not yet know the Lord: The word of the Lord had not yet been revealed to him."*

But once Samuel had that first encounter, where he knew he was experiencing the Lord, he was forever changed. Verse 19 says, *"The Lord was with Samuel as he grew up..."* and the very last sentence in the chapter says, *"...and there he revealed himself to Samuel through his word."* I know, you're thinking this is great, but this is OLD Testament. More like ancient history. Does this really stand true today? Yes!

John 1:1 says, *"In the beginning was the Word, and the Word was with God, and the Word was God."* The Word here is capitalized because it is a proper noun. The Word is the Son of God, Jesus. That is why the writer of Hebrews can say that the Word of God is living and active. Jesus is the Word. As you read the Holy Word of God, it does just want this verse says, IF you're willing to listen.

I'm not saying you won't experience God if you never open your Bible. I'm saying you will experience God in a way you never thought possible if you will get into your Bible. By being in the living Word, you are doing your part to develop a closer personal relationship with your Lord and Savior. He's just waiting for you!

Pause, Ponder and Pray

What keeps us from seeking God through His Word?

What might God want to "cut" from your life if you truly allowed the scriptures to be active in your life?

DAY 20

The Ways of the Lord are Right

"Who is wise? He will realize these things. Who is discerning? He will understand them. The ways of the Lord are right; the righteous walk in them, but the rebellious stumble." HOSEA 14:9 NIV

This is actually a riddle. Who knew! It's amazing what you find when you dig into God's Word! As I was reading in the Moody Bible Commentary it says, *"The point of the puzzle is not that the wise person will understand these prophecies, but that those who know them are in fact wise. (pg 1329)"* Think about that for a moment.

We won't immediately understand everything we read in the Bible, but at the right time God reveals to us what we need to know. Just because we might not understand what we read, doesn't mean we ignore it. We go ahead and believe what we read on faith, knowing that God's Word gives us wisdom.

Proverbs 3:13 says, *"Blessed is the man who finds wisdom, the man who gains understanding."* Where do we find this wisdom? Yes, we already said we find it in the Bible, but if we can't understand what we are reading, what do we need to do? We ask for understanding. James 1:5-6, *"If any of you lacks wisdom, he should ask God, who gives generously to all without finding fault, and it will be given to him."*

But back to the ways of the Lord being right. How many times do you think your way is right? I'm guilty of that. I think everyone should do things like I do them. My way is right! But I am not God; therefore, my ways are not always right. It is only after I have sought God's wisdom that my ways are right!

I know, I'm starting to sound like a broken record but, "Get in the Word!" Find out what's right!

Pause, Ponder and Pray

Do you always have to be right?

Why do you want to have your way? Have you truly searched the scriptures for the answer?

DAY 21

The Course before Us

"Therefore, since we are surrounded by such a huge crowd of witnesses to the life of faith, let us strip off every weight that slows us down, especially the sin that so easily trips us up. And let us run with endurance that race God has set before us." HEBREWS 12:1 NLT

Race day came for me as day 21 of this Devotional possibly has come for you, thinking it is all about to end. Are you excited or scared at the thought of what might come next? I know as my race day came, I really didn't know exactly what to expect. I had to rely on my training because I didn't know what the course looked like but trusted they had it marked out for us.

You might not be any surer of your course or what it looks like after these 21 days, but I hope you know the Course Designer better and know that you can trust His leading in your life.

This verse tells us we are surrounded by *a huge cloud of witnesses*. This would include all the great men and women of faith that we read about in the Bible, as well as the those we loved and admired that have gone on before us, can you hear their shouts of encouragement and joy? But we must remember that we also have a physical crowd of witnesses to encourage us here and now. They are encouraging us to, "*strip off every weight that slows us down, especially the sin that so easily trips us up.*" Sin weighs us down, both physically and spiritually. We need to be willing to do whatever it takes to free ourselves from sin. The NIV version reads, "*the sin that so easily entangles us*".

The picture that comes to my mind is getting your feet tangled up in rope or a vine. At first you just take a step or two, but quicker than you realize you're all tangled up! and the more you struggle, the more tangled you become. This is when you need a friend to come along side and help you "break free". We are told in Ecclesiastes 4:9-10, "*Two are better than one, because they have a good return for their work: If one falls down, his friend can help him up. But pity the man who falls and has no one to help him up!*"

We were not designed to run this race called Life alone. We need God and we need the brothers and sisters that make up the body of Christ to help us so that we can *run with endurance the race God has set before us* and when we finish the race, we will hear the words, "Well done, good and faithful servant!"

Pause, Ponder and Pray

On this 21st day, take an extra moment as you pause, ponder and pray and think about what tomorrow may bring. My prayer is that this is the beginning of something new for each of you, a deeper relationship with God, refreshed study habits and a new hunger for God's Word.

Who are the brothers and sisters in Christ that you look up to?

Who is a close friend that you can count on to help you?

Who are you encouraging?

Are you ready to "run with endurance the course set before you? Even if YOU can't see the twists and turns?

When the Lord lead me to write this 21-day devotional, I found that the actual time required to write and edit it took a lot more time than 21 days. What started out as a good idea, grew and stretched me in ways I never imagined and when it was over, I have felt a wide range of emotions because I thought the journey was over. But then again, the journey isn't really over, it's just the beginning! The beginning of something new that the Lord has yet to show me, but I know He will, because I trust Him!

Love, Hugs and Prayers,
Erica Wallace